Autumn Has the Most Important Job

poems by

Chelsea Locke

Finishing Line Press
Georgetown, Kentucky

Autumn Has the Most
Important Job

ACKNOWLEDGMENTS

Grateful acknowledgements are made to the following publications in which
these poems have appeared, sometimes in different forms:

Vida Amorosa Anthology: "Summer," "Mercy by the River Bed"
Untangled Rhymes Anthology: "Mercy by the River Bed"
Ink-O-Pedia Anthology: "Summer"

I would also like to acknowledge all of the love and support I got from my
husband, Daniel Smith. He believes in me even when I don't believe in
myself and has always been there to talk me through the tough times and
celebrate every time I've had something published. I love you.

I also want to make sure I thank my friends for cheering me on, most
notably: Lauren Proudfoot, Felicia Konrad, Sebi Priotese (who is a
wonderful poet), Anne Cain, and Toria Cordani.

Also thank you to Katherine Riegal for writing something so nice about my
book. I love your writing and I'm honored that you took the time to write
me a blurb.

Thank you also to Finishing Line Press for giving me this opportunity to
share my work.

Publisher: Leah Huete de Maines
Editor: Christen Kincaid
Cover Art: Chelsea Locke
Author Photo: Chelsea Locke
Cover Design: Elizabeth Maines McCleavy

Order online: www.finishinglinepress.com
also available on amazon.com

Author inquiries and mail orders:
Finishing Line Press
PO Box 1626
Georgetown, Kentucky 40324
USA

Table of Contents

Autumn..2

September...3

The Death of September 4

October 5

Pale Moon Witch...6

Hymns of the Grasshoppers...7

Hand Turkey 8

Winter 10

Gingerbread Men Can't Run Away 11

Imperial Sunshine 12

December Vacation...13

Your Hair Was Like Moonlight...14

I Blame the Groundhog 15

Spring..18

The Sound of the Seagulls Above the Wind....................19

Malachite Meadows..20

In the Morning Mist...21

The Willow Tree Will Keep Our Secrets...........................22

Mercy by the River Bed 23

Summer..26

Aureolin Blooms..27

Sea Glass 28

Whiskey on the Table...29

Urban Air..30

The Cicadas 31

Drink Deep..32

Dedicated to my father.
You taught me not to be afraid of the shadows
and always believed I could do anything.
I miss you.

Autumn

Autumn

Autumn has the most important job
when it balances night and day on a leaf tip
before waxing into the cusp of a scarf
pulled tight against
the oncoming cold. Unapologetic
oaks drop acorns onto my roof
to collect in my gutters
where the squirrels greedily gather them
to hide under my house
while muttering about the increasing chill in the air.
Evening brings me to sit on my porch
with mulled wine in my coffee mug,
hands warmed by the taste of fall,
and anticipation for the naked fingers of the trees
to call to the spirits waiting patiently for Halloween
so they may take advantage of the thin night
to visit their loved ones—so my father can be welcomed
through my door
to see what has become of the little girl
he used to put on his shoulders.
This is the time when magic slips into every breath
with the openness of a heart at the touch of their beloved
and the ripeness of the air brings
the need for apple spirits and pumpkin dreams
and a thankfulness for the harvested year
that lays nestled in the history of our ancestors
and now awakens in our souls.

September

September is my birthday month
and the leaves were drifting like snow
in a city that hasn't known snow since the 70s.
You stood behind me on the front porch
and I knew your warmth
like the blanket we would huddle under later that night.
There was a ripeness in the air
that signified pumpkins would be harvested soon
and gourds would be made to grin at trick or treaters in a month.
Are you ready for the spirits to grace our door?
In the city there are no bonfires to dance around,
no flames to illuminate our faces,
no snaking hands to conjure spells
as sparks drift towards the sky.
But magic would still seep into our lungs
as evening slipped over treetops to fall under the porch light
above our heads.
I could already smell it on your breath,
taste it on your tongue.

The Death of September

September died like the zucchini plant in the corner of our garden:
slowly, gently browning around the edges until it curled in on itself
to leave room for the crisp winds of October
to make their way through the slats in the fence
and into our kitchen window. Evening slipped across the yard
like the flannel sheets over our mattress,
like my hand down your arm as I eagerly pulled you
outside to watch the fireflies dance with the leaves
falling from the elm tree.
Are you as enchanted by the stars
moving just beyond our fingertips as I am?
Have you ever caught them in jars
to hold their winged constellations between your palms?
There were signals of love being transmitted through the dark
far more urgent than the ones that lazily seeped from our hearts
with the evenness of our breath.
They were at the mercy of the time it takes for two moons to pass
below the horizon before their search ends
and the grip of loss knocks them to the ground.

October

We met in early October
as the leaves turned over
and blazed across postcards, as apples
fell to the ground with the same thud
of a headboard against a bedroom wall,
as pumpkins ripened on vines
longer than the hangman's noose. Pulled taunt,
your arm dragged your body
to meet me under the ghosts
of harvest lanterns. Your calluses
wrapped around my hand like the neck of your favorite guitar
and I stood on pointe to follow you into the darkness
where we swayed in front of the jack-o'-lanterns carved early
by impatient children now dreaming
of candy that would never be as sweet as your tongue.
And Love, you tasted like fall and Halloween and happiness
and the last bit of magic before the sun rises to burn away
the sins your lips would leave smeared across my skin.

Pale Moon Witch

My pale moon witch writes with her hands,
etches phases into my cheekbones
with the push of the moon,
and pulls my fingers to her lips
only to press my palms against her eyes.
Softly, my future falls like smoke
from her tongue. There's a pressure
between my shoulder blades,
an omen settling onto the back of my lungs—
an offering. I am
slipping through sangria sunsets
and nights softer than her hair. My love,
when the dawn comes will you lay beside me?
Will you wrap yourself in my wings
and wait for the first stars
to inch their way through the light?

Hymns of the Grasshoppers

There's a gray sweatshirt I wear when the nostalgia slams
into my ribcage like the punch God landed when I was thirteen.
Defenseless. I was
thrown to the ground, knees bloody and palms
split down the center; today my chest still aches
with only the grasshoppers to repeat
their hymns in my outstretched palm. I remember
the stars were brilliant that night we'd laid out in the cold
and, too stubborn to fetch a blanket, I'd huddled
against your sweatshirt as though they would fall
without our breath
to push them against the velvet darkness. We'd tilted our faces up
and I had let the first prick of homesickness soak
between my eyebrows, longing
already working its way deep into my lungs. My father's smell
was as familiar as my own and I knew that
too soon I would lose him
like I'd lose the grasshoppers to the chill of late autumn
when the wind's blow would leave them
helpless in the dirt.

Hand Turkey

She is not tissue paper.
She is a haphazardly cut construction paper hand turkey
hung on the fridge every year for Thanksgiving
in her mom's house. Each year I would show up
at her door after Thanksgiving with my own mother
to sneak some food that was actually edible.
Her mom would scold me for knocking.
Only strangers knock. Family barges in.
I was the fourth daughter in the trio of siblings,
the extra plate at the table
even when money was tight. I never went hungry
in those days—my heart fed to the brim
with seconds of mashed potatoes,
another roll from the basket, more turkey
pulled straight from the wishbone.

Winter

Winter

Hysteria slipped from my temple
to nestle itself between the slightest twitch of my lips.
Zip codes are directly linked to mannerisms:
I'd separate my eggs, discard
the yolk, and seize the half-baked
ideals of suburbia between two fingers
before soaking them in my saliva.
Chewing.
Spitting.
Outside
it was changing, dying
as winter tried to etch its fingers into apple cores
and withered
to the tune of dead leaves drifting
    drifting
        drifting

Gingerbread Men Can't Run Away

Since it'd begun with your teardrop face
hanging over mine,
hair falling silken down your back,
it's only fitting that today I would love
your arms wrapped around my neck
while you whisper
strange words into my ear.
Gingerbread men can't run away
if you eat their legs first.
In my kitchen I don't have legs,
just my lips pressed to yours,
the scent of cloves and cinnamon in my nose—
the taste of ginger on my tongue.

Imperial Sunshine

Insufficient hands hack away at the mercy of the oranges
hanging gravid between the spines that are so painfully
patterned across their unruly branches. Almost elegantly
the fruit might fall on its own
with the readiness of a child from its mother's womb
after the initial frosts of winter begin
to push against the crumbling leaves
of the oaks standing vigil over the oranges slowly rotting
in the sand. But Florida is always as scorching as the lard sizzling
in the cast iron skillet your mom would use
to crisp the chicken for Sunday dinner;
the leftover heat could hold its fruit for another season—
selfish. We would slip under the fence
into the neighbor's yard to stand next to the dwarfed tree,
to steal a taste of Florida winter. We'd hold the setting sun
in our hands with the intent to peel away it's protection
and relish in its nectar.

December Vacation

December clenched my chest
with the eagerness of the mulled wine to stain your lips
with cinnamon
and honey. I'd held you that night
when you'd slumped into my arms
with the enthusiasm of a child on Christmas morning:
eyes brighter than the afternoon sun
on the fresh snow outside our window.
Those evenings always brought spiked tea
only slightly cooler than your palms
against my back and the last light from the fire smoldering
in the fireplace would play charades on the far wall
while I played them across your stomach.

Your Hair Was Like Moonlight

You've aged
since the night I'd cradled the phone to my ear
and held your rosary in my hands.
Every winter I pray
for my hair to turn the same shade of moonlight as yours—
like the moonlight that hung over your shoulders
that night we'd braved the cold
to watch the eclipse
lengthen the shadows from the cypress trees
to create the nothingness below our feet.
Did you grasp at that darkness
in the hopes that it'd save you?
Did you know that time was handing you memories
it never intended you to be able to keep?

I Blame the Groundhog

It's still winter when a rodent hands out predictions
with the same confidence you'd read my fortune
in the stars above our heads
the night we snuck out of our bedrooms
to lay at the edge of the orange grove.
I didn't question you
or the sureness of your hand in mine
while you pointed out Sagittarius
and boasted that the Babylonians worshiped him
as a god. There was always an easiness in your words
that lulled me into believing
Spring might come early this year
while the reality was that Winter had always been
nestled between your lips
as surely as I saw my shadow in the moonlight.

Spring

Spring

Spring always blows in madness
before the April showers
while the northern children play
in the slush after the last bell rings,
releasing them onto the street.
I would stand vigil
over my seeds wrapped in damp paper towels
in my kitchen window;
waiting for the first sprigs of life
to create roots where I'd had none before.

The Sound of the Seagulls above the Wind

Seagulls voiced their need
for the crisp winds of early spring
to warm into air worth their spread wings
and readiness to fly. We stood
with the sand stinging the backs of our claves
and our hair in our faces
deciding if it was worth daring
to dip our toes in the waves.
The view from the shore was tremendous. Still,
all oceans criticize the scope of their onlookers
and I was no different, casting sidelong glances
over the foam collecting at its edges like great scars
left from when the surf and land met,
my skin recoiling against the sea spray.
But you—
you spread out your arms like an egret spreads its wings
and I swear I saw you fly.

Malachite Meadows

April sat heavy in my hands like a grapefruit
already starting to spoil. She was
laughing at something over my shoulder
and I knew that if I chanced turning
I'd have to turn back to her
inching further out of my reach. Tonight
we stand at the corner of evening and night
and my heart beats to every pulse of the moths wings
as they wait for the light above our heads
to let them cast shadows on our faces.
My breath comes out in time with the streetlights
blinking on—one by one. The world unravels
to let the dark creep between blades of grass,
turning yards into fields of malachite.
There were great meadows there once, before the houses.
When I'd moved here we'd roll in the wild flowers,
face the sun no matter the direction it'd take us.
Do you remember? I'd kissed you then. Now
with the light gone and only the moths to play witness
and our silence to stretch between us,
I turn away.

In the Morning Mist

After the rooster crows from two houses over
and the neighbor's kids walk through the morning mist
like zombies dragging their waning childhoods in their backpacks,
the bees stick to the coral vine along my fence
like it's the only thing anchoring them
to their niche in the ecosystem. There is an importance
in their movements
as their hind legs become gravid with pollen
and they gently move
from one eggplant flower to the next;
a goodness
in their biology that muses the voice in the creative
matching of DNA from plant to plant
that only man can so rudely interrupt.

The Willow Tree Will Keep Our Secrets

There's a certain appeal to the bruise colored haze at the bottom
of a six-pack. She sat on the kitchen floor, knees bent
out at acute angles, shuddering shoulder
blades pressing against skin
until that fine human film split
and she fell—split down the center
like the bottom of the Colorado mountain valleys we'd hiked
last spring. The skin of her cheeks would flush
in the brisk mornings and
I, alone, learned every shade of tension
stretched through her shoulders
when she'd bend
over to wash her hair in the stream—
like the willow tree bends: graceful
limbs reaching to touch a quivering reflection.

Mercy by the River Bed

May found us hiding in Colorado under willow and boxelder trees,
dipping our toes in the river while the Rockies still wore snowcaps
and tried to hold onto the last shreds of winter.
You threw pebbles wrapped in worries into the current.
I leaned against a boulder that dwarfed me and the anxieties
still shuffling through my fingers—nervous energy
like the air before the storms
back in Texas. I still waited for you to touch me first
and pull me into the sleeping bag
in your jeep. I watched you lay back
on the sandstone, chunks of quartz peeking out
from the surrounding rocks to shimmer like trapped flames
in the afternoon sun,
and thanked God
for this small mercy that lay down by the riverbed.

Summer

Summer

She lingered over her martini,
an olive floating gracefully in the gin,
vermouth and humor sitting dry on her tongue.
The summer evening slowly inched itself across the tablecloth
until the light from the candle at the center
hindered its crusade to bring on the dark.
I ran my hand over the flame, letting it lick the dent of my palm,
inching it further down
until the quick pain reminded me of that first pinprick of love
the night we'd met. *Do you remember*
the earthy smell of the apples slowly rotting under the leaves?
The world altering itself beneath our feet?
There was a sense of urgency back then, a need
for hastened fingertips
and my lips to always be pressed to yours,
skin rubbed in raw emotion until it burned like kindling
in the night. Your eyes were golden
under the lanterns, your hands pale birds
swooping over your plate.
In that moment my skin burned for the ocean
of your curls across my hips,
the charm on your necklace to brush against my thigh,
the warmth of summer waves to pulse beneath my skin.

Aureolin Blooms

Florida showers leave the sun to hang hopeful in the sky.
Even under the safety of the umbrella, it left
its reflection to bloom aureolin under your fingers
at the first drops of rain—
like when the artists had spread their paint
across the watercolors
hanging inside the café;
bright splashes of hope to contrast the blues.
Across the table, you uncross your legs, open
like the orchids flourishing on the windowsill,
lounging in the humidity
while it collects in your hair and trickles down your neck
like the most bewitching of poetry.

Sea Glass

Knob kneed and pale,
I glow
before the waves with toes painted green
like the world through a piece of sea glass, my vision hazed
and calm. Your thumb presses my fingers
like the tactile press of a keyboard's
steps towards the fully formed sentences
I can't quite seem to finish.
The storm on the horizon is electrifying.
It drowns out my breath with each rumble
echoing over the waves
and we know we should leave,
move to safety,
but the water is the most intense
shade of you.

Whiskey on the Table

Whiskey on the table could please
even the most demanding follower of Freud.
You are the painted flower on my living room wall;
never wilting
past the curling of its edges
in the Florida humidity. In summer
we'd loved your father
for the coal he lit out back of your house where
we would lay on old sheets to watch the stars
blinking on like the light in your bedroom window
to let me know you were still awake.
Love is the interrelatedness of all things irrational
and I'd waited for your eyes to open
and understand the reason behind
the hastiness of my hand to hold yours
while pulling you into the tree house.
With each stumble I would reach for you
like the silken petals of the sunflower towering above our heads,
wanting to see if it could outshine your smile,
knowing full well
that your shooting star would run through everything
to keep us safe.
Even my hand fell silent
when your fingers pressed into my arm to drag me into the night
to watch Pluto through the eye of your telescope, but
I was only interested in the warmth of your breath
evaporating in the heat
before it had a chance
to taste the perfume of your hair:
apple, like the pie we'd baked
late the night your parents left us
with your sister.
That night I'd extended my heart towards yours
like the whiskey I'm pushing across the table:
unsure of the world
behind your eyes.

Urban Air

The urban air weighs heavy on my chest
like my hand when I try to press my anxieties back
into my sternum. Outside the blue jays call to each other
in a pitch that leaves my fingers pressing to my temples
as I try to stop the throbbing that pulses with every beat of my heart.
This used to come easy;
my fingers relishing in the tactile press of the keyboard
would lull me like a baby gently rocked in its father's arms.
My father held me more than my mother—
or at least that's what I remember.
Bipolar is genetic. Did you know that?
I am different than she is. A different type.
    More subdued.
        Second string.
If you stare through the screen your eyes will focus
on the squares caging you from the vines creeping up the window
    panes,
        but it won't save you
from the smell of the neighbors smoker
that makes you hunger for the food beyond the fence.
There the songbirds serenade each other
like the waves do to the sand. My ankles
ache for the steady rhythm of the water to soothe my heartbeat,
the warm salt air to expand my lungs,
the vastness of the Atlantic
to steal away the panic burrowed between my ribs.

The Cicadas

Cicadas skip years.
I skip stones
across the high tide
engulfing my ankles.
Have you ever held
a piece of limestone
smoothed by the push
and pull of the moon? I have
cut my foot on oyster shells
reaching for one
just below the surface
while the buzzing
and clicks of the bugs
pushed at my back,
drowning out the sound
of your shadow.

Drink Deep

Drink deep. The ocean
is gray like the sweatshirt tucked away
in the back of my closet. There are trails
between the dunes
where the grasses brush against my hand
as I step against the wind
and salt. My edges are as salted as the rim
of the glass in my hand
and there is tequila on my lips
and a burning sweetness in my stomach
as I sway with the blanketflowers
fighting against the storm. *I held my ground*
when the sea swell called to my feet,
didn't I? I don't know
where reason lives
or the incidents that leave me asking
for the water to close itself around my shoulders
with the warm kindness of my father. But
if I stand just right
I can see his shadow on the sand
telling me to go back inside.

Chelsea Locke holds two bachelor's degrees (one in Anthropology and one in English with a concentration in creative writing) and a master's degree in Anthropology. She has been published in Thread Literary Inquiry, Dark Poets Club, The Sock Drawer, Flora Fiction, The Broken Plate, Yellow Arrow Journal and numerous anthologies. She is a pole dance fitness instructor, a pole dance performer, and has a less interesting day job. She currently lives in Tampa, Florida, in the United States.

Chelsea has lived in Florida for most of her life, but is an avid traveler. She uses her experiences as inspiration for her writing. She loves to attempt to capture moments in vivid detail so she can share what she sees with the world.

CPSIA information can be obtained
at www.ICGtesting.com
Printed in the USA
JSHW050351220722
28357JS00003B/189

9 781646 628919